Glow-in-the-Dark Animals

FLASHLIGHT FISH

Caitie McAneney

PowerKiDS press.

New York

Published in 2015 by The Rosen Publishing Group, Inc.
29 East 21st Street, New York, NY 10010

First Edition

Editor: Katie Kawa
Book Design: Katelyn Heinle

Photo Credits: Cover Borut Furlan/WaterFrame/Getty Images; cover, pp. 1–24 (background texture) olesya k/Shutterstock.com; pp. 4 (flashlight fish), 16–17 Norbert Wu/Minden Pictures/Getty Images; pp. 4–5 (coral reef) John A. Anderson/Shutterstock.com; pp. 6–7, 14–15, 20 (squid) Ethan Daniels/Shutterstock.com; pp. 8–9, 22 Visuals Unlimited, Inc./David Fleetham/Visuals Unlimited/ Getty Images pp. 10–11 (fish) Frederick R McConnaughey/Photo Researchers/Getty Images; p. 11 (bacteria) Laguna Design/ Oxford Scientific/Getty Images; pp. 12–13 TOM MCHUGH/Photo Researchers/Getty Images; pp. 18–19 (zooplankton) Roland Birke/Photographer's Choice/Getty Images; p. 19 (shrimp) Konoka Amane/Shutterstock.com; pp. 20–21 (jellyfish) Richard A McMillin/Shutterstock.com.

Library of Congress Cataloging-in-Publication Data

McAneney, Caitlin, author.
 Flashlight fish / Caitie McAneney.
     pages cm — (Glow-in-the-dark animals)
 Includes bibliographical references and index.
ISBN 978-1-4994-0121-9 (pbk.)
ISBN 978-1-4994-0122-6 (6 pack)
ISBN 978-1-4994-0120-2 (library binding)
1. Bioluminescence—Juvenile literature. 2. Fishes—Adaptations—Juvenile literature. I. Title.
QH641.M29 2015
597.147—dc23
                                   2014029743

Manufactured in the United States of America

CPSIA Compliance Information: Batch #CW15PK: For Further Information contact Rosen Publishing, New York, New York at 1-800-237-9932

CONTENTS

A Light in the Dark.............................4

Dark Dwellers 6

Blending In...................................8

A Glowing Relationship 10

Strength in Numbers.........................12

The Best Defense 14

Making More Flashlights 16

Confusing Prey 18

The Future of Flashlight Fish 20

Fun Flashlight Fish Facts 22

Glossary 23

Index..24

Websites 24

A LIGHT IN THE DARK

Can you imagine how dark it gets deep in the ocean? It's very dark, and animals that live there have **adapted** to it. One animal that has adapted to life in the darkness of the sea is the flashlight fish. Parts of its body glow in the dark!

There are three main species, or kinds, of flashlight fish. All are small, dark fish that are known for the glow underneath their eyes. One species lives in the Caribbean Sea. Two others live in the Indo-Pacific region, or the area covered by the Indian and the Pacific Oceans.

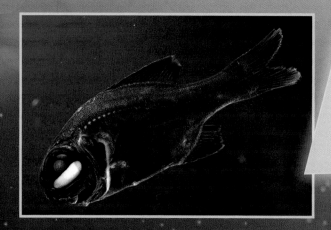

NEWS FLASH!

Flashlight fish are also called lantern-eye fish. That makes it easy to get them confused with another glowing fish—the lantern fish!

The Indo-Pacific region has coral reefs that are home
to many species of fish, including flashlight fish.

DARK DWELLERS

Flashlight fish live in saltwater **habitats**. While flashlight fish don't live in the deepest parts of the sea, they stay about 1,300 feet (395 m) below the surface when the sun is out. This helps them stay safe from predators. They travel to **shallow** waters at night to find food.

These glowing fish live in large schools, or groups. They hide in dark places along coral reefs. Flashlight fish love the dark so much they only come out at night. That means they're nocturnal.

Flashlight fish hide in underwater caves during the day. The darker the cave, the better!

NEWS FLASH!

Flashlight fish don't even like light from the moon. If there's no moonlight, they sometimes swim closer to the water's surface.

BLENDING IN

If the flashlight fish didn't glow under its eyes, you might not be able to see it! Its body is almost black, which helps it blend in to its dark habitat. If you saw one in the ocean, it might just look like a glowing dot. The glowing dot, which is shaped like a bean, is actually an **organ** called a photophore (FOH-tuh-fohr).

Most flashlight fish grow to be only about 5 inches (13 cm) long. The females are bigger than the males. Females even **protect** males if bigger fish come along. They scare the bigger fish away with their light!

The light from a flashlight fish can be seen from over 100 feet (30 m) away!

NEWS FLASH!

A photophore is an organ that produces light. Other glowing animals have photophores on different parts of their body. Lantern fish have photophores close to their eyes and tail fins.

A GLOWING RELATIONSHIP

What makes flashlight fish glow? It all starts with a relationship, or connection, between the flashlight fish and the glowing bacteria around them. These bacteria are bioluminescent (by-oh-loo-muh-NEH-suhnt), which means they can produce their own light. They do this through a **chemical reaction**. Bioluminescent bacteria float around the ocean, but they're so tiny that we can't see them. However, the bacteria sometimes settle down to live inside another living thing.

In the case of the flashlight fish, the glowing bacteria settle inside the photophores under their eyes. The bacteria gain a home, and the fish gain their flashlights. Everyone wins!

NEWS FLASH!

Other deep-sea and reef fish are bioluminescent, too. One of these is the anglerfish, which lives in even deeper waters than the flashlight fish.

A relationship between two living things where both things benefit is called a symbiotic relationship. Flashlight fish and glowing bacteria have a symbiotic relationship.

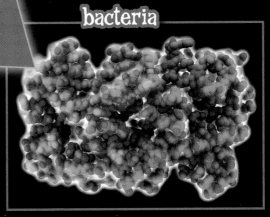

bacteria

STRENGTH IN NUMBERS

Flashlight fish schools stay together as they look for food and protect themselves from predators. They use their lights as a **defense** against animals that try to attack them.

Imagine you're a big fish, trying to hunt a flashlight fish. Suddenly, you see a huge school of flashlight fish, blinking their lights. You try to follow them, but you can't. They're swimming in a zigzag pattern. They often swim in one direction with their lights on, and then swim back with their lights off. You get confused and lose track of them completely!

Flashlight fish can turn their lights on and off by covering their light organs with a film. They can also turn their photophores so they can't be seen.

THE BEST DEFENSE

How successful are flashlight fish when it comes to escaping predators? Scientists believe they're great at it! Flashlight fish are almost never found in the stomachs of other fish.

You can tell if a flashlight fish senses danger by the speed of its flashes. When it's safe, a flashlight fish only blinks a couple of times a minute. But when a flashlight fish feels it's in danger, it can blink its light from 50 to 70 times a minute to confuse predators. The speed of its flashes also warns other flashlight fish that predators are near.

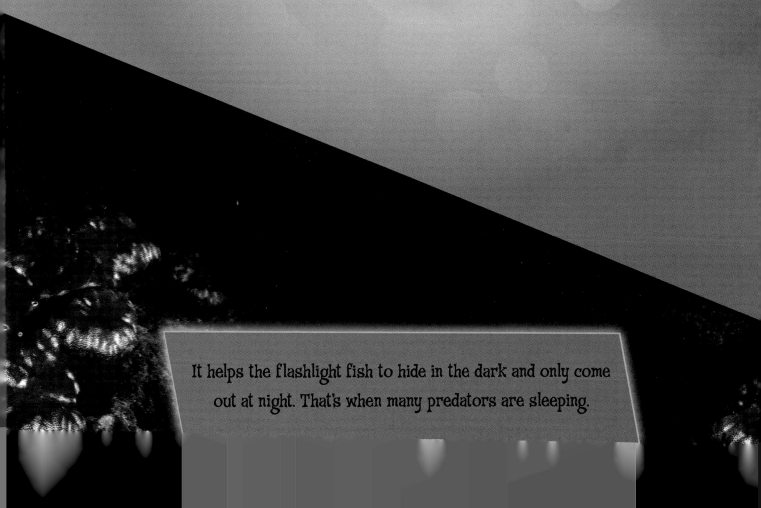

It helps the flashlight fish to hide in the dark and only come out at night. That's when many predators are sleeping.

MAKING MORE FLASHLIGHTS

Scientists believe flashlight fish also use their lights to **communicate** with one another. One time this comes in handy is during mating. "Mating" means "making babies."

We don't know much about flashlight fish mating. That's because during the day, flashlight fish are too deep in the water to study them. Scientists do know that flashlight fish make babies by **spawning** in the open ocean. Flashlight fish babies, called larvae, live in caves and cracks in rocks while they grow. These are the same caves adults live in during the day.

Scientists believe flashlight fish don't glow until they're adults. They aren't born with glowing bacteria in their photophores.

CONFUSING PREY

Flashlight fish may be small, but they're great hunters! They use their lights to catch **prey**, which include small fish and zooplankton. Zooplankton are tiny animals that float around in the ocean. Zooplankton aren't great swimmers, so many animals eat them.

Flashlight fish use their light to **attract** floating zooplankton. The zooplankton float to the light, and that's when the flashlight fish eat them. Small fish sometimes swim up to flashlight fish, trying to eat the zooplankton. They only see a floating light, so they don't know a predator is waiting. Flashlight fish catch these fish by surprise!

NEWS FLASH!

When flashlight fish move from deep waters to shallow waters for food, it's called vertical migration. "Vertical" means "up and down," and "migration" means "moving."

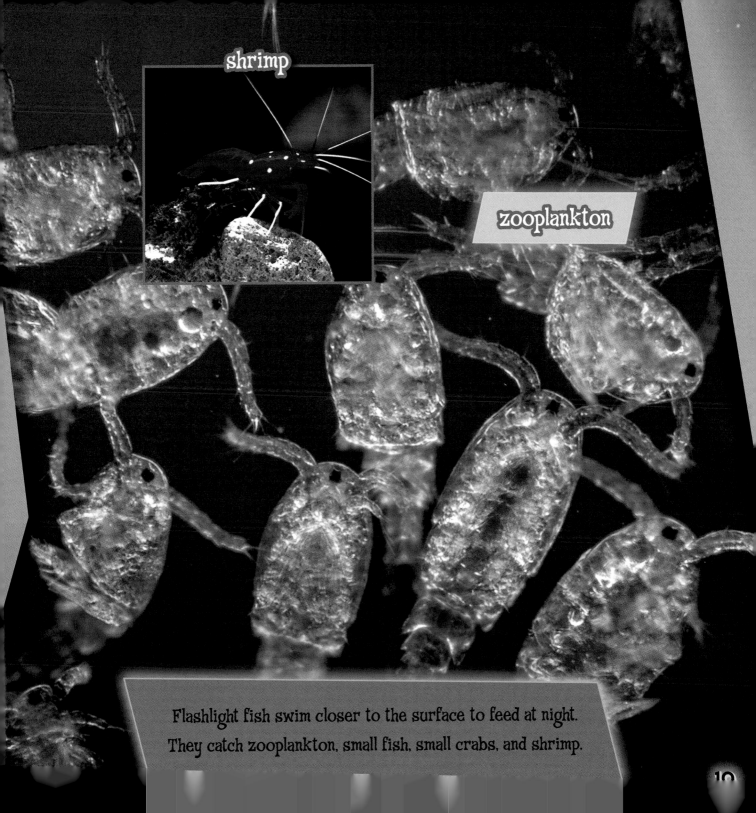

shrimp

zooplankton

Flashlight fish swim closer to the surface to feed at night.
They catch zooplankton, small fish, small crabs, and shrimp.

THE FUTURE OF FLASHLIGHT FISH

While other ocean fish are collected by the thousands to be used as pets, flashlight fish are rarely caught. That's because they live deep in the ocean and only come out in the dark.

One way people can keep flashlight fish safe is by keeping their coral reef habitats clean. You can help by using less water and not supporting companies that dump waste in the ocean. These glowing fish are not in danger yet, however. They hopefully have a bright future ahead of them!

squid

Can you think of other animals that glow? Some other bioluminescent animals include fireflies and glowworms, as well as certain squids and jellyfish.

jellyfish

NEWS FLASH!

Coral reefs are home to a quarter of all sea creatures. Humans hurt coral reefs by overfishing, adding to **climate change**, polluting the water, and mining coral.

FUN FLASHLIGHT FISH FACTS

1 Flashlight fish glow the brightest of all bioluminescent animals.

2 Flashlight fish grow larger the deeper they live in the ocean.

3 The longest flashlight fish are almost 1 foot (30 cm) long.

4 Some schools of flashlight fish have up to 200 fish in them.

5 There are billions of glowing bacteria living in the light organs of each flashlight fish.

6 Some fishermen take out flashlight fishes' photophores and use them to help catch other fish.

GLOSSARY

adapt: To change to fit new conditions.

attract: To cause to come close.

chemical reaction: The process by which matter is changed after coming into contact with other matter.

climate change: Change in Earth's climate, or weather, caused partly by human actions, such as burning coal and oil.

communicate: To share ideas and feelings.

coral reef: A line of coral skeletons that forms in warm, shallow ocean waters.

defense: A means or method of protecting from harm.

habitat: The natural home for plants, animals, and other living things.

organ: A part inside the body that does a job.

prey: An animal hunted by other animals for food.

protect: To keep safe.

shallow: Not deep.

spawn: A way some ocean animals produce young by letting loose eggs and male cells in the water.

INDEX

B

babies, 16

bacteria, 10, 11, 16, 22

bioluminescent, 10, 20, 22

C

Caribbean Sea, 4

caves, 6, 16

coral reefs, 5, 6, 20, 21

D

defense, 12

F

females, 8

H

habitat, 6, 8, 20

I

Indo-Pacific region, 4, 5

M

males, 8

P

photophores, 8, 9, 10, 12, 16

predators, 12, 14, 15, 18

prey, 18

S

schools, 6, 12, 22

spawning, 16

species, 4, 5

symbiotic, 11

Z

zooplankton, 18, 19

WEBSITES

Due to the changing nature of Internet links, PowerKids Press has developed an online list of websites related to the subject of this book. This site is updated regularly. Please use this link to access the list: www.powerkidslinks.com/gitda/flash